The Cat and the Bird

Ron Holt

 My name's Mary. I'm eight years old. My hair is black. My dress is yellow and my shoes are red. This is my bedroom.

 This is Tom. He's my cat. He's three years old and he's black and brown. He's on my bed. He's a bad cat.
 Miaow.

 Tom! You're a bad cat. This isn't your bed and this isn't your room. Your bed is in the kitchen. Out you go, Tom! Out!

 Miaow.

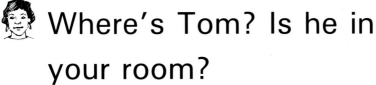 Where's Tom? Is he in your room?
No. He isn't in my room now.
Where is he? Is he in here?
Yes, he is. He's under the table.

 This is my bird. He's yellow and his name is Tweet. He's one year old. Tweet is in his cage. The cage is in the living room.
 Tweet! Tweet!

 Tom? Where are you?
 I'm here. I'm on the table.
 Where's Mary? Where is she?
 She isn't here. She's in her bedroom.
 Mary! Help! Tweet! Tweet!

🐦 My cage is on the floor.
Ha! Ha! Look at Tom!
He's in my cage.
🐱 Miaow...I'm in Tweet's cage. Tweet is on the table. Come here, Tweet!
🐦 Where's Mary? Mary!
Help! Tweet, tweet, tweet!

 Tom! You're a bad cat!
You're in Tweet's cage.
Come here!
 Miaow.
 Poor Tweet. Are you OK?
 Tweet, tweet.

 Tom! You're a bad cat.
 Miaow.
 Where's Tweet now? He isn't on the table. He isn't under the table. Where is he? Oh! The window's open. Tweet's in the garden!
 Miaow.

Tweet! Where are you?
What's the matter, Mary?
Where's Tweet, Mummy?
Isn't he in his cage?
No, he isn't.
Look at the apple tree.
Is that a yellow apple?
No. It's Tweet!
Tweet, tweet!

 Where's Tweet's cage?
It's in the living room.
Get the cage. Quick!
Tom! Stay there!
Daddy is in the house.
I'll get Daddy.

 Hi, Mary!
 Hi, Sam!
 Tweet isn't in the house.
Where is he?
 Ask Tom.
 Where's Tweet, Tom?
 Miaow.

 Mary, tell me. Where's Tweet?

 Look in the tree. What's that?

 It's an apple. A yellow apple.

 No, it isn't. It isn't a yellow apple. It's Tweet.

 Come on, Sam. Come with me.
 Where?
 Into the house. Let's get a ladder. Let's put the ladder beside the tree.
 OK.
 Get on the ladder, Sam.

 It's no good, Mary.
 Come on, Sam. Climb the ladder.
 OK.
 One more step.
 There you are.
 Now catch Tweet.
 I can't catch Tweet.

 Hi, you two!
 Hi, Dad!
 What's the matter, Sam?
Are you OK?
 I'm OK, but Tweet isn't.
 Where's Tweet?
 He's in the tree . . .
Next to Tom!

Where's your fishing net, Sam?
 It's in my room.
 Go and get it.
 OK, Dad.
 Tom! Come down!
 Here's my net, Dad.
 Thanks. Come here Tweet. There! Put Tweet in his cage, Mary.

 Is Tweet OK, Mary?
 Yes, he's OK now. He's in his cage.
 Is Tom OK, Sam?
 Yes, he's OK now. He's in my fishing net. He's a catfish.
 Ha! Ha! Poor Tom!

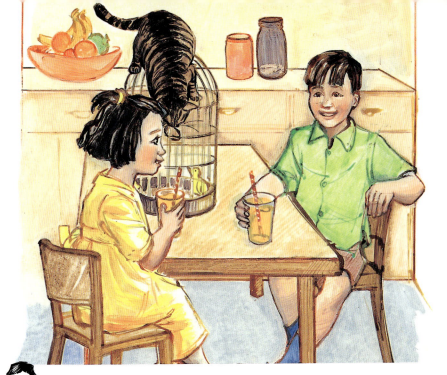

Here's some orange juice.
Thanks, Mummy.
Here's some milk for Tom.
Where is Tom?
He's behind you. He's on Tweet's cage.
Tweet, tweet.
Tom! You're a bad cat. Get down.
Miaow . . .

A game
Draw a line from Tom to Tweet.

There's a mouse house
In the hall wall
With a small door
By the hall floor
Where the fat cat
Sits all day,
Sits that way
All day
Every day
Just to say,
'Come out and play'
To the nice mice
In the mouse house
In the hall wall
With the small door
By the hall floor.

And do they
Come out and play
When the fat cat
Asks them to?

Well, would you?

John Ciardi

A puzzle

Across

1
3 (bird)
4 (cheese)
6 (trees/bush)
8 (ink blot / stone)
10

Down

1
2 (table)
5 (orange)
7 (apple)
9 (chair)
11 (net)